Copyright 2012 Lesley Fletcher (text and artwork, cover, design )

Copyright 2012 Sebastien Assoignons and Lesley Fletcher (Thru the Window, Mermaid, Peace)

Copyright 2012 Ahmad Osaili and Lesley Fletcher (5 Pillars)

All rights reserved. No part of this book may be used or reproduced in any manner whatsoever without written permission from the author except in the case of brief quotations embodied in critical articles and review.

*5 Pillars of the Gypsy*  ISBN  9 780986 533242

For any inquiries please contact:

Lesley Fletcher at   Lesley@lesleyfletcher.com

www.lesleyfletcher.com

# 5 Pillars of the Gypsy

*Art & Verse*

*by*

*Lesley Fletcher*

This is my heart.

*'Eva Dancing' Water Colour, pastel, mixed*

"To everything there is a season, and a time to every purpose under the heaven: A time to be born, and a time to die; A time to kill and a time to heal; A time to weep and a time to laugh; A time to love, and a time to hate; A Time of war, and a time of peace." Prime Minister Rabin

&

To which I would like to add: I personally hope this is a time to heal, to seek, to love and especially a time of lasting peace. The above quote is exactly right with the exception of a missing gem ... "It is time now to choose to lie down in defeat or dance to your heart's content." Lesley Fletcher

*5 Pillars – Water colour with enhancement by Ahmad Osaili*

# *Pillar I*

"Encore of a Beginning"

- The Mission
- The Soldier
- The Promise
- Emergence
- Time
- Lone Dancer
- Legacy
- Spoken
- The Flame

*"The only way to make sense out of change is to plunge into it, move with it, and join the dance." Alan Watts*

*"I have but one lamp by which my feet are guided, and that is the lamp of experience. I know of no way of judging the future but by the past." Patrick Henry*

# The Mission

Allow me to recharge my existence,

Join the music in the air,

Bind emotions up in packages,

And throw them out to sea.


Waiting for the tide to bring

Something back anew,

Useless memories left

To sink in the big blue.


Childish thoughts please stay with me.

With those I will not falter.

Sadness, jealousy and grief,

Just stay inside the water.


Rip the poison threads

That keep my senses so confined.

Replace the spoils, cast-asides

*With grounded peace of mind.*

*As I toss dead roses to the depths*

*Along with sad occasions,*

*Sweep back to me my great big sea,*

*Soft leaves and petals only.*

*Rejuvenate in sunshine*

*What once was lost in snow.*

*The days of past, the months,*

*The years I no longer want to know.*

*In their place please put seconds,*

*Minutes – hours,*

*Allowing me to live again…*

*I know it's in your powers.*

*Dear God, I've travelled far to sit*

*Beside Your pond,*

*Be baptized by your touch,*

*Regain momentum, feed the aching, starving*

*Self so much.*

*I'm peering at a bottle now.*

*It's rising with the tide.*

*Have all my rambling*

*Prayers been answered*

*By the note enclosed inside?*

*Wading in to gather up*

*The bottle to my breast,*

*Enclosed with arms crossed tightly*

*As the water comes to crest.*

*With shaking hands I fumble*

*For the message you have sent,*

*Thru the Window – Re-worked on photography by Sebastien Assoignons*

And read the note at least ten times

To understand just what you meant.

You said:

"Child, it's time to ask you to throw caution to the wind,

to laugh, to sing, to dance, to rejoice in a multitude of things.

Time, it waits for no one.

Let me set that record straight.

Your time on earth is given

Only as guidance to my gate.

Once inside I'll welcome you

In the style in which

You lived,

With purity and selflessness,

With efforts passing limits.

And all those thoughts and feelings

You have thrown here

From the shore

*Will no longer darken, hurt or hold you.*

*You won't need them anymore.*


*But now understand, you*

*Cannot toss those memories afar today.*

*They'll stay with you to*

*Steer and veer life's obstacles*

*Along the way.*

*When earthly life is over*

*And the angels bring you here,*

*That's when you get*

*To shed that load.*

*All sorrows disappear."*


*Folded now inside my mind*

*That note did just the thing.*

*God sent my way that day*

*With words as clear as spoken.*

*In doing so I was renewed,*

*As was my main ambition.*

*To sing and dance, rejoice in life,*

*...I accept this simple mission.*

*Join Me – Water colour*

# *The Soldier*

The strain of wartime music,

Played softly in the background

In contrast with the present,

The harsher, modern sound.


Swaying to the softness,

Escaping here and now,

Simple times, simple ways,

A song of love and hope.


'La Vie en Rose' could only be

So sung in this reality

By none other than the

Stranger as he moves up close to me.


Sensing more than seeing does,

Eyes sweep to catch this sight,

But nowhere is this singing man

Who greets me from the night.

With sultry words and voice so clear,

Defying ages absolutely.

Backwards, downwards, my eyes sweep

To finally catch a glimpse.


Lyrics filter through the air

With sweetness and with grace

Before I see the memories

That are etched upon his face.


Faded blue by time that's past

His eyes seem not quite focused,

'La Vie en Rose' so softly sung,

Alluring, not unnoticed.

*Poppies – Monoprint with chine colle*

*Swirls of present pass us by*

*As minutes seem like hours,*

*And in his song I melt myself,*

*Taking in his powers.*


*A grand finale does not come,*

*Though one arm moves up slightly.*

*'La Vie en Rose' has played out,*

*His audience delighted.*


*The war it took its toll I see,*

*Somewhat so encumbered,*

*Peaking out of his shirt so white*

*Reveals to me his numbers.*


*And yet with time and through the pain,*

*He sits to serenade.*

*A lovely woman all alone,*

*Appreciates he came.*

*To sing, to talk, perhaps to dance*

*So slowly and with innocence.*

*The chair rotating round the floor,*

*Forgetting all, remembering more.*


*The past crawls backwards,*

*Bright lights glare, present moment over.*

*'La Vie en Rose' contained for now*

*By he who is a*

*Soldier.*

*Victory Dance – Monoprint with chine colle*

# *Promise*

Who is this woman that I see

Who conjures up the man in me?

Against the odds, against the miles

I am deeply stricken by those smiles.


The poetry that leaves my pen

Is for her heart complete and open.

I trust the naïveté; I see it in her eyes.


I'm half naked and exposed

And fear nothing of the lack of clothes.

She will not stare nor compromise

Oh so careful with those eyes.


Exposed I am, exposed and free

To bare my soul for her to see.

I tease her endlessly today

Because I need her laugh to stay.

*I want to show her part of me*

*My passion, joy, humility.*

*Pride eclipses, minutes pass*

*I know she watches – I hope entranced.*

*Today I let her know once more*

*In better words than twice before*

*The generation that separates*

*Is all so easy to negate.*

*The flattery that is forthcoming*

*Is real and true and from within.*

*Those years would all but disappear*

*If all her dreams would bring her near.*

*Those dreams of souls and ones of peace*

*The ones that cause her face to crease*

*And bring the water to those eyes*

*The musing dreamer never dies...*

*She's surreal in her heart's beliefs*

*A heart sincere (to my relief).*

*My exposure is for her to keep.*

*It's soul to soul when next we meet...*

*Swallowed - Monoprint*

*Emergence – Water colour*

# *Emergence*

Taking ego to the air tonight
Mixed with sweet perfume.
Nothingness is out of sight
Spring flowers start to bloom.

Old age tried knocking at my door
Finding out there's really no one
Cus I'm out taking in the sights
Of an evening not ignored.

Walking proudly, strolling tall
The swishing of my dress
Strokes my thighs as
I feel a soft and warm caress.

For once I choose to see the eyes
That follow in my wake,
Oh yes he's cute and even sweet
So I adjust my gait.

The conversation is so trite
I've heard it all before
A million times repeated
There is surely more!


This emergence means so much

But only just to me; I see
Blending with the normalcy
Of others' careless whispers.

While whispers speak in volumes
To the moon up with the stars,
They glide off me, falling loudly
On the grass they leave their scars.

Perhaps to rise once more
On a less fussy one than me
They'll likely do the trick
And seem like destiny.

But I, my ego so intact
Won't get swayed by less than more
Continue on this sultry walk
I'm sensing more in store.

# *Time*

The hands of time are messing

With this crazy head of mine

One minute time is racing by

Next minute quiet lull.


The clock has guided oh so many

Through the ages, over eons

It's the one that says –

Grow up, get married

The one that won't stop streaming.


The one that ticks so rapidly

When a woman needs a child;


The one that slows so stubbornly

When that baby is inside;


The one that picks up pace

*As that child approaches school;*

*The one that (for some at least)*

*Blurs September until June.*

*The clock that shows the final moment*

*As a mother you're not quite needed*

*Then pedals backward one more time*

*To prove that theory wrong.*

*This is when the clock decides*

*(Whether fast or slow)*

*And somewhere in this lifetime*

*I am sure – I know.*

The clock will balance out its passing

And the right time will prevail...


Meanwhile ticking loudly by

At the pace it's meant to be.


Until that time is oh so right

And we have both begun

To realize as time goes by

It chooses how, so loudly

To demonstrate its power

And take over the controls.


The choice is not with me

It is only with time – you'll see.

*The Swan – Monoprint with chine colle*

## Lone Dancer

She dances all alone now
Where once it counted four.
They'd make their silly entrances
Through the kitchen door.

From the look that lights her face
Through loneliness held within,
She holds on to sweet memories
Not likely to wear thin.

Passing windows
One – two – three
She dips and swirls unbound
At the sweetness of
The freedom
In the music she has found.

There is no shyness
In her steps
No holding back emotions
With eyes closed tight
Smiling wide;
Serenity her right.
Her head tilts backward, Shoulders roll, Torso sending vibes
Exposing outside to her soul

*Dancing Spirit – Water*

*Reliving her past lives.*

*Through the darkness into lightness*
*Any given night*
*Peer in to see the spectacle*
*This truly awesome sight.*

*With her music*
*And her memories*
*Clearly all exposed*
*Of her gracefulness of movement*
*From her head right to her toes.*

*The crowds now gather nightly*
*To hold a piece of what she owns*
*No snickering or hiding*
*As she dips from highs to lows.*

*Partaking in the watching*
*Alights wonderment, surprise*
*In her innate ability*
*To surrender to the skies.*

*Departing now her audience*
*Is touched with gratitude*
*To have shared this carefree*
*Woman's dance...*
*In her solitude.*

## *Legacy*

If I was told

"Rewrite your life,"
I would not edit it.
Instead I'd glorify

The good and
Cross out the negative.


The red line strikes
Would be so few,
The words allowed to flow
To tell great stories
Deep and true and still
Allow for sorrow.

It's challenges that make
Me proud, and they
Are overcome
And when left to steep
In time and sleep,
Illuminate me some.

The dawn breaks gently

On the pain; now so much time has passed

*Eva's House on the Lakeshore - Water colour*

*And that filing cabinet,*
*Oh so precious,*
*Has numbered out and slashed.*

*The drawers remain*
*So full and bursting,*
*And the folders*
*Marked with 'L'*
*Hold love and laughter,*

*Life and longing.*
*There are no such things in hell!*


*&*



*Reroute those thoughts.*
*Reroute that fear*
*And all that don't belong*
*And fill that drawer's capacity*
*To hear the angel's song.*

*The day seems clearer*
*Than the night.*
*And so it's meant to be*
*That the systems of our thought processes*
*Are meant to let us see.*

*And hide I won't*
*Nor strike – nor cover*
*The past cannot be buried*
*But rather used to rectify*
*And give us back the power.*

*Power fragile – power strong,*
*Power wide and far,*
*Power making offerings*
*Of gentleness, desire…*

*Knowledge deep and*
*Knowledge clear*
*Become our legacy,*
*A legacy that holds no boundaries.*
*It's made of you and me.*

*Circles of Life – Monoprint with chine colle*

## *Spoken*

When the words you crave are spoken
And you don't believe they're true,
You've surely reached a day
That seems (to me) most overdue.

When those words caress your being
And resonate so clear,
And yet you somehow doubt that truth,
The truth you've longed to hear.

When you ponder them once over
And ponder five times more
And begin to see the realness,
You have youth upon your door.

The youth thought lost to sorrows
Is once again renewed,
But this time with the wisdom
Of all that has ensued.

*1st Love - Monoprint*

# The Flame

As the flames die slowly with the night,

Extinguishing the day

Smoke silhouetting through the quiet air

Taking shape of snapshots

Of memories, not long forgotten,

Igniting sweet desires instead;

Of candles burning every night

And romance in the atmosphere;

The scent of rare patchouli

Teasing in the shadows;

Nostrils slightly flared.

Soft rock music fills

The gaps between silent knowing glances

Mismatched glasses toasting

Filled with cheap Chianti

As the bottle gathers wax.

Cracker crumbs fall in between

Well-worn cushions of the couch.

Baby-doll pyjamas barely

Bothering to cover.

&

The night falls inaudibly.

Stealing eyes' content and gentle smile

Baccarat crystal shattering

Falling from her fragile grip,

Onto the shining marble floor

Mimicking a blood bath

Is Châteauneuf-de-Pape.

Slumped in true abandon

Of this life she's earned to live

Returning to her heart's true love

If only in her vivid final dream…

Lasting an eternity

Meeting her rebirth

Embossed upon her soul

As the next life starts de novo

And the flame again ablaze.

*Fire on the Water - Monoprint*

# Pillar II

"Discoveries of a Universal World"

- Now
- The Pilgrimage
- The Understanding
- Assalam Alaikoom (Peace be Upon You)
- Bridges

"I love you when you bow in your mosque, kneel in your temple, pray in your church. For you and I are sons of one religion, and it is the spirit." Khalil Gilbran

"Power does not lie in physical strength but in an indomitable moral will." Gandhi

"Nothing is so strong as gentleness and nothing so gentle as real strength." Frances de Sales

# *Now*

Now when the heavens cry
I cry with them;

When the sun shines
I fly;

Now when the songs
Are heard

I smile;

And in the silence

I think;

Now when the music plays
I dance;
And the freedom envelops me.

Since losing you
I have found me.

I detest the trade
That was made,

Yet I soar higher
Every day.

And every day...
And every day...


I am sadder by the day.

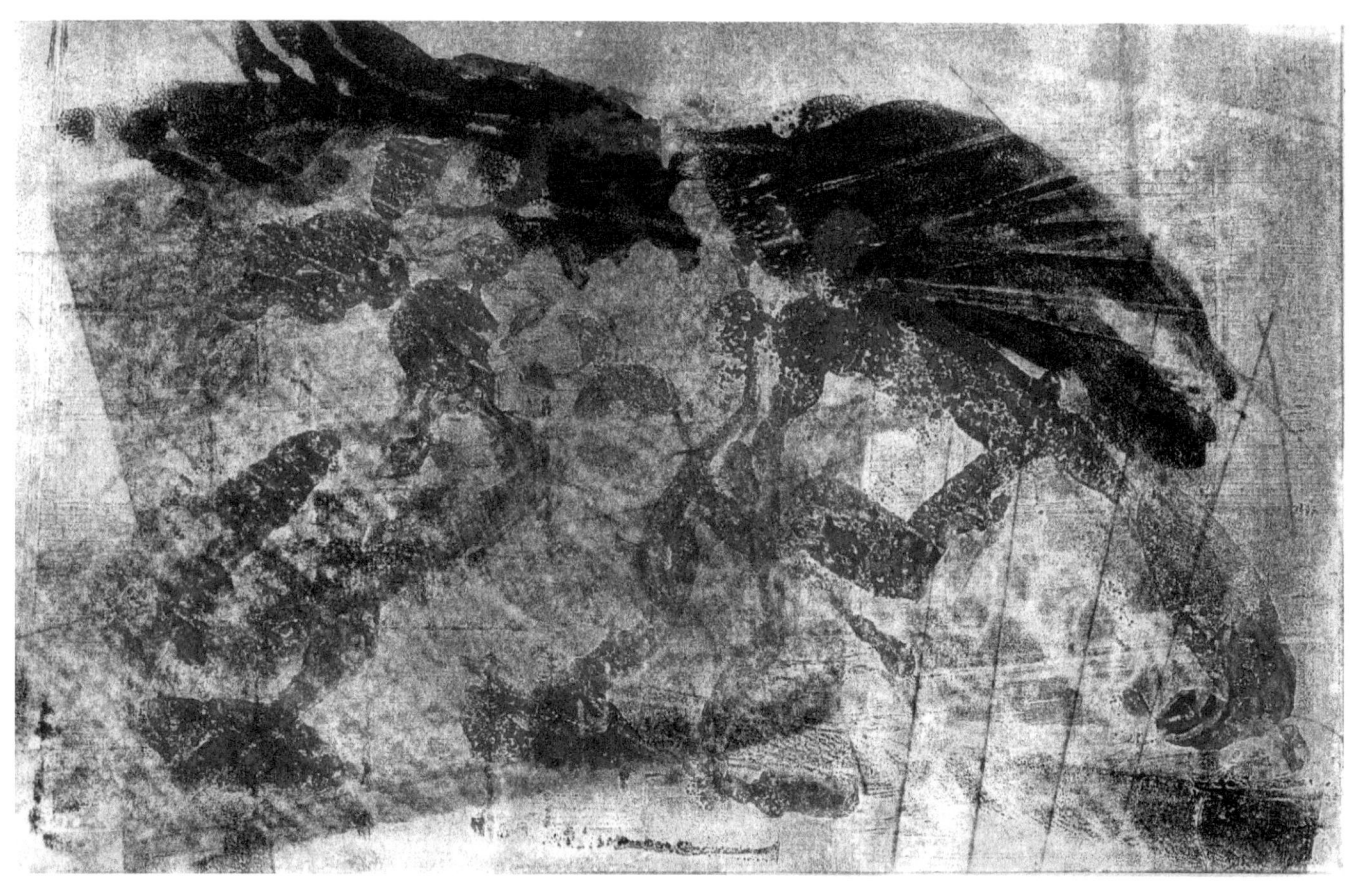
*Wings of Intaglio – Artist proof*

# The Pilgrimage

The desert sands are blowing

Wind so dry and soft

Feels as though the truth

Is in the air; aloft.


For all of us to listen

With silence and in awe

Multitudes of pilgrims

Reminded of their flaws.


Shrouded now as all the rest

Seeking, searching, walking blessed

To realize with certainty

We are His honoured guests.


Left at the fork

We take our leave

From others heading right.

Superiority is our guidance

Knowing what we seek

*Will endure from now*

*Until eternity; leaving*

*Non-believers weak.*


*Circles in the desert sand*

*Are not a common thing*

*Murmurs start up slowly*

*With love and light; anticipating...*


*All the books of preaching*

*Cannot replace this quest.*

*Words are but a guideline*

*It's heart and soul that*

*Say it best.*


*So to heart and soul of all mankind*

*We succumb and give our energy;*

*A group of us believers*

*Angel of Peace - Monoprint*

*(In) one God is all we see.*

*Returning from this sacred place*

*There walks a different group*

*One who holds the secret deep inside*

*Who knows the answers too.*

*Who travelled far and sacrificed*

*To generate the power*

*Of spirituality so strong*

*It has not a single name*

*Instead it has one hundred.*

*Encompassing all holiness*

*All writings by the verse*

*It's God above*

*Who walks with us*

*Humans here on earth.*

*Taking in the universe and*

*Working with all might*

*True beings seeking wisdom*

*Letting in his light.*


*Spreading hereon forward*

*The gifts they have to share*

*In solitude and masses*

*Contentment in the air.*

2nd Peace - Monoprint

## *The Understanding*

I am an oxymoron
And deal with it each day.
You see, I hate
The haters in the world and
Won't indulge in their play.

Being me, I take the time
To step into their shoes
And gander from the
Other side.
But I have naught to lose.

From minds of hate come
Words that spew
With spit and with it phlegm.
They are meant to insult,
Belittle and tear up other men.

I hurl with those thoughts and words
And twist right inside out,
And finally end up screaming back,
My voice beyond a shout.

I hate you all you haters,
Who spin our goodness to your side,

Who use the work of angels

And force them to collide.
Who set apart all goodness,
Peace and harmony to satisfy
The anger, pain, injustice that
You feel.

And through these words and actions
Be what they may,
The oxymoron lives in most
And will not go away.


I love the love of lovers,
The opposite of sins.
Rose-coloured glasses suit my face,
Forcing the look in.

Who am I to judge the lovers,
Sinners; in between,
Parked out in the suburbs
With oceans in the seams.

&

"You cannot know the meaning of the hatred I've endured."
Said one great man who suffered
Through the casualties of war.

*Misunderstood – Mixed collage*

"To move my family out from a country we adored,
To save the children from the bombs
And death and terror by the score.

"To live in shackles though appear
Free to do just what we will.
What does it look like, woman,
As you peer down from your hill?

"It's not the way you think it is
You've not walked in my shoes...
My family is safe for now
But so much has ensued.

"The blasting of hand grenades
Now feel like simple firecrackers,
Machine guns belting at our home
Has come – it hardly matters.

"Our food you see is on our plates,
And we must eat our dinner.
Too many times the bombs
Have struck and
Not produced a winner.


"So packed our bags,
Each one of us,
And split our kinfolk far and wide
Until we can go home again
When our enemies subside.

*"Judge not our anger
Nor our hatred of
Injustice to our people,
Take a look a whole lot deeper
And listen to us as we speak.*

*"Feel the pain that's recent,
And know the pain that's past.
Then divulge to me of love and peace
And harmony that lasts.*

*"Cus talk is cheap as
People say – it's action that is heard.
But action gives us casualties
And hurts our people more.*

*"I'm not saying you are wrong
Or suggesting you think different.
Just realize
There's going to be a
Residual effect
Even of the kindest individual...*

Turquoise Eye - Monprint with chine colle

*And we too pray for the day*

*That peace is in the wings,*
*And if hate's a sin we look*
*To God to forgive us of those things.*

*"For we are human beings*
*In a world that's just not fair.*
*And sometimes in our hearts*
*We find that we don't care.*
*Beyond our own survival,*
*We sometimes do not think.*

*"We are oxymorons too,*
*In an elaborate web of hate.*
*We are oxymorons*
*...absolutely, just like you...*
*We find we hate the haters too."*

*Housing Block #5 - Monoprint*

## Assalam Alaikoom
### (Peace Be Upon You)

The call for prayer mixes
with the rooster's call.
They complement each other.

The stars still glow through the
darkness,
And all the house is still.

But for the sound of chai boiling on the stove
And the quiet snores.

Silence follows with
No interruption as the
Stillness fills the quiet.

Nothing seems too foreign
Except for the
Absence of noise and
The presence of God.

# *Bridges*

I look to building bridges,
To build them strong,
To build them fast, as time is running rampant
To build from history.

But, alas,
The history just repeats itself,
And bridges keep collapsing,
And still no rules apply,
And still no absolution exists.

But, alas, instead
I look to build a smaller bridge,
A bridge I can adhere to,
And in this act is progress
No matter how so minuscule.

And so, alas, in keeping
It made a tiny dent
In my heart and in theirs,
And a solitary bridge still stands
And history is rewritten.

Albeit it grand in one's own eye,
It makes a tiny difference.

but
If all would build a simple bridge,
Then we could all change history.

# Pillar III

"Realities of a Life"

- The Sea – The Shore
- Numb
- Rise and Fall
- Saving Grace
- Spirit Inside

"A question that sometimes drives me hazy: am I or are the others crazy?" Albert Einstein

"Our task must be to free ourselves by widening our circle of compassion to embrace all living creatures and the whole of nature and its beauty." Albert Einstein

## The Sea

Where those who dare

Dive deep

And set a history

For themselves,

Who feel the rush, the high

Of depths so low

Adding to the wonder.

The water and the tide,

The time and the breath,

The prayers and the spirits,

The peace and the harmony.

With first the earth

And then

The air

And finally

The deep blue sea.

*Sea of Good Wishes - Monoprint*

## The Shore

And as I listen at the shore,

The lake makes an ocean sound

And brings me closer

And brings you near.

Water of Aquarians,

Of fathers,

Of lovers,

Of earth,

And of hunters.

Where lions go to

Cool and sip,

Where humans bathe

The dirt away.

And as I listen at the shore.

It brings me closer  - And you near.

# Numb

Numbness is feeling too

It radiates her eyes.

Nothing hurts her anymore

Not even wretched lies.

She's numb from life;

Supposedly pain-free

Appears it from the outside

But inside we can't see.


Like the duck that floats the water

She looks calm now, most serene

But peer beneath the

surface

It's quite a different scene.

As water flows right off her back

Protective outer feathers shine

*Oh but what of those webbed feet*

*What of her racing mind?*

*½ Way There – Acrylic, gouache*

# *Fall and Rise*

It must be getting close now
To disappearing time

Where all the love
Surprises, thoughtfulness
Are stored for the
Next round.

Sinking into your self-destruction
Letting sorrow take its hold.

Growing weary of your life.
Hiding all from those
Who know.

Closing up your heart
Not letting them see
The worst you have to offer.

No matter what they say
Handling it alone.

Trusting only you to do so.
Fighting the urge to
End it all.

Recognize yourself;
The core of strength

That you have used before
to see you through
the madness
that consumes
each waking hour.
Quit your job
A thousand times
And wonder at your boss
Who won't accept you're done.

Now worry how it is
That they can see the sorrow.
What makes him care
About a life
That has no certain meaning.

Is it that smile
That mystery

Is it those eyes
That show

Is it that heart
That beats
Or the angel
in your soul?
The one that dares to surface
Despite your solo plight
Or the one that offers vision
To the man who lost his sight?

*Still grasping days*
*And searching*
*In the past*
*provides some guidance*
*to reality that sits within*
*Awaiting months to wash away.*

*Then...one day*
*It is over.*
*To the surface*
*you shall rise*
*And gasp for air*
*And fill your lungs.*
*With breath you are afloat.*

*Sail above the earthlings*
*Share with them your humour.*

*Give over sacred parts of you*
*Remember not the cold.*

*Drink in the glorious sunshine*
*Lie down in warming winds*
*Frolic in the massive waves*
*Rejoice in joy and sing.*

*Play music loud and often*
*Dance to the sound it makes*
*Celebrate that God*
*Has given*
*Another chance to you.*

*Then one day...*
*Remember those*
*Who loved through*
*The darkness*

*Who love you now*
*Despite witnessing*
*Your unravel*

*So even*
*when you're all alone*
*Celebrate with*
*Those people too.*

*Look back to that self-despair*
*Pensive, solemn and aware*
*Thanking each (and every one)*
*For all their love and care.*

*I am Human - Monoprint*

## *Saving Grace*

*The haggard face looks weary.*
*Life took its toll too early.*
*The eyes that once were sparkling*
*Growing squint against the sun.*

*Revealing lines more so*
*Than just short months ago.*

*Drawing eyes to yours to question*
*The age of one so very young.*
*Demands a concrete answer to...*
*What have you been through, son?*


*Disappointments etched in creases*
*Hunger crawls the surface,*
*Searching for a reason*
*That only he can fathom.*

*Dreams dare not be dreamed*
*By someone sinking*
*Into thoughts malnourished*
*By a life that has since passed.*

*Starving for contentment*
*Intimate without*

*Trust in God seems not enough*
*In this his time of drought.*

*Tenderness and loving care*
*Are right within his reach*
*But deems himself unworthy*
*And lies down in defeat.*


*&*


*The eyes to soul have wandered*
*And he's picked out one or two*
*To trust with all those secrets*
*That may just hold the clue;*

*To a lifetime of fulfillment*
*A family and a place*
*His to own forever more*
*Will be his saving grace.*

*The Church Window – Monoprint with chine colle*

# *Spirit Inside*

Human spirit lies deep inside
While the outside seems explosive
The peace the spirit brings
Is the purpose of its focus.

To human eyes it is not visible
(the very soul inside)
It's the tie that binds
The spirit to the ever moving mind.

The soul is fed from elements
Our existence is exposed to
The spirit, heart and soul
For only one to have and hold.

To human eyes it is not visible
(the beating heart that races)
As all elements that do collide
Leave no marks nor traces.

And so to your spirit you must trust
To fix the damage (maybe) done
Rely on you, your heart, your soul
To feed that mighty spirit some.

# Pillar IV

## "Mindful of an Imagination"

- Angel Path
- Mighty Unicorn
- Tangled
- Fairy Love
- Damaged Heart
- Loaner – Kinda
- The Healing
- Dance with the Devil

"Do not go where the path may lead, go instead where there is no path and leave a trail." Ralph Waldo Emerson

"True wisdom comes to each of us when we realize how little we understand about life, ourselves, and the world around us." Socrates

`I believe in everything until it`s disproved. So I believe in fairies, the myths, dragons. It all exists, even if it`s in your mind. Who`s to say that dreams and nightmares aren`t as real as the here and now? John Lennon

# The Angel Path

I stepped on all the stones
To make my way across the stream
Not to feel the water
On my toes and in between.

The stones were laid out perfectly
In zigzags and in rows
That's when it occurred to me:
They know the path I chose!

Suddenly those simple stones
transformed before my eyes
Taking on illumination
That shot up to the skies.

The water formed a circle
That was very clear to see
It took the shape of halos
And lit the crooked path for me.

How lovely of my angels
To guide me, hold my hand
This simple little journey
Now deserved a band.

'Transcendent Angels' Acrylic

And suddenly from nowhere
Sweet music fills the night
If it wasn't so delightful
I'd surely get a fright.

Then the lights changed colours
Flashing softly off and on
With shades of turquoise, orange, pink
I heard the angel's song.

Quite enchanted with the tune
I danced with some abandon
In the moonlight with the stars,
Nothing weighed me down.


Floating now across the water
Taking in the light show
Why this happened here and now
I intend to know...

One day I think I'll ask them
One day when I am bored
But right now's not the right time,

I'll let the reason stay ignored.

*The Crooked Path – Monoprint with chine colle*

# *The Mighty Unicorn*

Four corners of the earth sent their finest representation with thrilled anticipation – rushing, pushing, spying, over-garbed formality, drenched with perspiration – to be greeted by the gracious queen,

Who put aside her tireless tasks to hold the hands of landed guests in hers, assuring them, with charm and dignity, intelligence and beauty, that her home was theirs.

Vast delight lingered long after greetings paused, allowing thoughts of unfolding circumstances to brew,

Pondering, perhaps, what may be a crystal-clear reality answering life's ancient mystery.

The whole taking place in her small country: misunderstood desert lands, rare green mountains, history entrenched with richness, the basis of mankind.

Where the call for prayer five times a day reminds the people of their debt and promises to family roots and God himself.

All the kerfuffle worth the price of travel via any route as now the grandest spectacle unfurls.

Yes! Continuing for days to see the vision grazing the horizon, leaving witnesses hungrily enamoured: love at first sight collectively.

 Each of those who query, who speak in hushed and secret tones dispatching vast conspiracies – the grandest hoax to date – deny it in this instance.

The entire held instead fast, furious, attentive – not hungering for food or drink or camaraderie – spellbound by the performances of the mighty unicorn.

Arriving in terrific droves, the unicorns crammed the surface, free at last to taste fresh air.

Speckling the horizon, horns encrusted proving years of digging, winning liberty to perform rehearsed ballets for the world to flatter.

*Into the Mystic - Monoprint*

Eyes alert, snouts bursting through the surface salt, not quite hiding smiles as they formed their clever shapes. Gliding into crosses, stars and crescent moons; forming words of wisdom, in every language that exists, legitimizing fairy tales and books of God alike.

Accounts of mourning and demise of their fine species gone by returning to the earth from which they vanished all those years ago.
The terrain that held their history, glory, fantasy without the foresight it now had.

"Be gone, naysayers," they seemed to cry. "Be gone and fill your vast reports to agencies not slightly worthy of all we have to share.

Human beings thousands strong will testify our presence – we're back: sharper, faster, stronger, wiser – united and uniting."

Five days and nights they danced and whirled designed to entertain the masses until, in fair-haired glory – manes, tails and horns of solid gold – they set off the salty sea with ease and galloped through the crowds.

With smooth comfort and in chorus their lovely wings unfolded; leaving miracles in their midst, the unicorns took flight.

Spectators stared in gratitude; privileged, they applauded; spontaneous in laughter, embracing one another.

Waving, cheering frantically as the beasts lit up the evening sky, splitting into smaller groups aimed for earth's four corners.

Circling just one more time, they hovered, basking in what was declared to be an encore of their encore.


Beginning then in earnest, they set out to meet their destiny – demonstrating for the human race to grasp new visions of the Dead Sea and with it endless possibilities.

*Life of the Unicorn - Monoprint*

## *Tangled*

When a sea of good wishes
Washed to the shore
No one quite saw them
No one quite cared.

Within the tangled mess
There glittered some diamonds,
But no one slowed to see them,
And no one slowed to care.

The wishes and diamonds
Had long been ignored
Until you came along,
And you wanted more.

So you stopped by the seaside
And listened and stared
And gathered the wishes
And diamonds. You dared.

Now when you walk,
They shine in your eyes,
Glow through your smile
And reside in your heart
For all to enjoy.

*But still no one listens,*
*And still no one cares.*

*If only they knew*
*What you had to share.*
*If only they'd dare.*

# Fairy Love

There are fairies in the air today.

They run and skip and jump so high.

It seems like they can reach the sky.

They zoom like tiny lightning bugs

And tease the children oh so much.


They picked this horrid place, you see,

Because I think they followed me,

To sprinkle children as they play

On pavement 'tween the cars astray.


Their father, see, is in the bar

And they were left inside the car.

When they notice him emerge, the fairies float away

To hover over other kids who need them as they play.


The fairies followed me once more to see me home and safe.

And just as I had reached my door one flew in my face!

She told me of a secret for only me to hear…


She told me that they stayed with me and always would appear.

So now I look for children who need some fairy dust

To help them grow up softly – for me this is a must.


The parking lot was not so bad as cars pulled in and out.

The fairies kept the children safe and all without a shout.

I'm grateful on this day to see the children playing oh so freely

And fairies soaring high and low over those they love so dearly.

*Fairies – Water colour*

*She told me that they stayed with me and always would appear.*

*So now I look for children who need some fairy dust*

*To help them grow up softly – for me this is a must.*

*The parking lot was not so bad as cars pulled in and out.*

*The fairies kept the children safe and all without a shout.*

*I'm grateful on this day to see the children playing oh so freely*

*And fairies soaring high and low over those they love so dearly.*

# *Damaged Heart*

A heart that's raped and damaged
By the guilty and the strong
How to best describe it
By the innocents and wrongs.

Shattered into tiny bits of crystal
When it falls
Combining hurtfulness, no mercy
Signalling nothing full at all.

Until the sun alights those tiny shatters;
Memory ignites
to take it back to days concluded
To evenings colourful and bright.

Build back the pieces one by one
With slight and shaken fingers.
Careful to adhere original
Old heart lingers.

Resist again to fall downtrodden
A heart broken with fragility of glass
Knows well that once again (it)
Will crack repeatedly as past.

*Many bruises, many fractures*
*So much reparation*
*Bound to come undone again*
*With the smallest of occasions.*

## *Loaner*

So you've nabbed yourself a bad boy

Complete with fresh tattoo

You've gone and done it

Anyway – though you know it is taboo


And you laugh away the warnings

To enjoy his winning grin

Scoff at those in all their doubt

Because he's just the thing

To bolster up your ego

Ensure your sex appeal

You gaze at him with eyes

That say "Pinch me are you real?"


Walk beside him, pride intact

Letting stares bounce back to owner

You've nabbed your bad boy

Even though he is a loaner.

Man in the Mirror - Collage

# *Kinda*

You were in my head today,

Your breath upon my body,

It kinda caused my hips to sway

As I climbed my flight of stairs.

You were in my body today,

I trembled from inside.

It kinda caused my head to sway,

Like you lived inside my mind.

You were in my heart today,

The tugging causing trouble.

It kinda caused my body to sway.

I was thinking of you double.

You were in my soul today

For only me to feel.

*It kinda caused my heart to sway.*

*It kinda brought you nearer.*


*You were in real life today,*

*The elements combined.*

*Head, body, heart and soul they swayed*

*And made up for lost time.*

*The Tango — Water colour*

# The Healing

My skin – it seems on fire with the feeling of your touch.

I swim in paradise sinking further in your kiss.

To lift the weight that held me once to another man

I look to you to bring out in me exactly who I am.


The stars are shining through the clouds; darkness in the wake.

The shivers felt so slightly are only from your touch.

The breath that leaves your lips is powerful and warm.

The lust that seeps our bodies is only what we long.


The moon, the sky seen from this spot are aphrodisiacs,

As though this coupling needed more...

I'm not so sure of that.

Oh, fantasy, it has come true upon the seaside now.

Your hands have touched the soul in me.

We've reached the here and now.

The dream it has no ending as it had no start.

It feels as though the man in you has entered in my heart.

The eyes that show me tenderness, so obvious you feel,

Has me knowing, after all, it's possible to heal.


But healing souls is such a task no human should it lay.

I look to God for guidance in my judgment here today.

And God he looked upon me and said "Do what you will."

*The Mermaid – Re-worked photo on photography paper – original photograph by Sebastien Assoignons*

*He understands past carnage versus pleasures now instilled.*

*And so it's passed right back to this soulful human here*

*Who lies upon my body and erases all my fear.*

*Serious may not apply to this very moment*

*For no contracts are instilled.*

*Instead, we know, we're certain.*

*Let the tide flow where it may,*

*Indulging in the flesh.*

*The language of the universe*

*Are words that suit it best.*

*Let the love that sways so freely be not the hurting kind,*

*But rather, love that's meant to feed the body, soul and mind.*

# Dance with the Devil

The devil grabbed me by the leg

Trying to bring me down

To a level at the time so tempting

As revenge already held me.


"If it's revenge you seek – believe in me."


He flashed me photos

He whispered truths

He dangled live emotions

Before averted ears and eyes.


Afraid, alone with weapons

Forced upon me

I took hold of my senses

Staring blind at his attack.

"What will I do to pacify you?"

I mewed against all will.

His piercing blacks flashing


Will power, guts and chill.

"Payback for 'sins' as you people claim

Is not to be ignored but rather conquered.

 Redemption  gained !"


"I'll do as you say – divulge the route."

His placidity still contained.

 I stood  innocent, succumbing

To his power he stood subdued and pensive

Wondering my sway.


The grip on my leg formed

To a "sweet" caress

Taking every single morsel

Not to cry out in my distress.

*Resurrection - Monoprint*

*"Dance with me tonight*

*Under the silvery moon.*

*Throw your body soul and heart*

*And I will aid revenge*

*With a rampant start!"*


*With that he pushed his lips on mine*

*To seal the wicked deal.*

*Weak-kneed with fright, anticipation*

*He took this to his ego*

*Chest swelling with the promise*

*Of victory on his part.*


*And that is how it came to be*

*On the beach in paling light*

*Romantic overtures perceived*

*By only him and me.*


*Yes, I danced with the devil*

*Pretending abandon*

*With grace and so with ease*

*And he in turn was eager just to please.*


*While during the dance*

*My blinders fell loose*

*Evaporating all remnants of*

*The age-old curse.*

*Cavernous - Monoprint*

As the music took pause

I remained in his grip

Notes entered my heart

Giving back life.


Pounding gently once more

I heard my heart swish

With innocence vanished;

It directed a symphony of angels and trumpets.

Hosts of heavenly sounds.


With this I was certain

With this I was strong

No revenge would I seek

The devil was wrong.


"Devil be damned"

I managed to utter

As he struggled and sputtered

As he fought hard to stay.

*A mighty bolt of lightning*

*Fell onto to the sand*

*Sticking the devil*

*As I twirled and danced.*


*"Yes, Devil be damned!"*

*I roared at his head.*

*As he tumbled and shook*

*As I took him for dead.*


*Alone I danced*

*Alone and free*

*Of all revenge*

*Of misery.*

# Pillar V

"Musings of a Gypsy"

- The Gypsy
- The Gypsy Continues
- The Gypsy is Found
- The Gypsy Restored (the finale)

"Man is lost and is wandering in a jungle where real values have no meaning. Real values can have meaning to man only when he steps on to the spiritual path, a path where negative emotions have no use." *Sai Baba*

"An individual has not started living until he can rise above the narrow confines of his individualistic concerns to the broader concerns of all humanity." *Martin Luther King, Jr.*

*The Back Path – Monoprint, chine colle*

## *The Gypsy*

When the winds of change
Grow silent
And the gypsy
Is confused
And there is no
Other avenue
She wishes
To pursue,

Then the hands
Of time
Will falter
And the spirit
Disengage,
Then no longer
Will her
Soul survive
No fire in her gaze.

She lays her head
To bed at night
Somewhat mystified.
The bed is
Warm and solid.
The house
Is cool and calm.

*Then why is it*
*This gypsy*
*Feels not*
*That she belongs?*

*Will that magic wind*
*Return*
*And fire up her sails*
*So she can feel*
*Her soul again*
*With whatever*
*That prevails?*

*The night will*
*Turn to dawn*
*For just*
*Another day,*
*Another day*
*Of nothingness*
*Without the winds*
*Of change.*

*Perhaps this day*
*She'll take*
*Her leave*
*And*
*Feel her freedom*
*Once again,*

*Or perhaps*
*Enjoy just*
*One more night*
*In her*
*Environment*
*So strange.*

*When she finally*

*Takes her leave*

*Of all that is at stake,*

*She will not glance backward,*

*Leaving nothing in her wake.*

*&*

*Enchanted Forest – Monoprint with texture and chine colle*

## *The Gypsy Continues*

Then the winds of change blew rampant

As they rustled through the trees

Did hit the gypsy solidly

And knock her to her knees.


She raised her eyes to heaven

And thanked her lucky stars,

For the strength she had been given

To separate those bars.


If it had been

In years of past

The ship would set to sail

Instead she waits

By the in box

*For tickets via email.*

*Her destination is unknown*

*As she contemplates her choices.*

*The gypsy sure of just one thing...*

*Her singing heart rejoices.*

*When she leaves that life behind*

*For twenty-seven days,*

*The universe must guide her*

*As she stumbles through the haze.*

*And sure enough those angels*

*Who had brought her to this point,*

*Choose to float and fly with patience,*

*Helping God anoint.*

*Ever grateful, still uncertain*

*Of the journey she is on,*

*The gypsy takes advantage of*

*The freedom she has longed.*

*Only she will recognize*

*When the reason comes to surface,*

*Why the need for solitude;*

*What is her very purpose?*

*Wandering without an anchor,*

*Charmed by all in sight,*

*No one sees the gypsy's pain*

*Or thinks she's earned the right.*

*The Cleanse in Abstract x's 2 – Water colour*

# The Gypsy is Found

The gypsy's found her sails again

Eating strictly from the sea.

The lifstyle once beloved

Has lent her remedies.


No mercury does poison her

Nor complicated strategies

At one with God, effortlessly

It's life the way it's meant to be.


Another land awaits her still

Does strangle in its hold.

She'll go back with some reluctance,

*But owning, now, her soul.*

*Sweet memories remind her*

*Of simplicity and freedom,*

*Adaption to the here and now*

*Living in God's kingdom.*

*Awaiting for the day once more*

*That lights her inner fires;*

*Grateful for the time she's given*

*Fulfilling deep desires.*

*Yesterdays are over and*

*Tomorrows fill her now*

*As she sits filled with all placidity*

*Upon life's messy bow.*

*Mixed Emotions - Monoprint*

# *The Gypsy Restored (Finale)*

I am awakened by the call for prayer, my hands already facing upwards in submission, having stayed that way all night. I dare not stir too much as I think without my usual logic that any movement in high temperatures could possibly exhaust me into sleeping late.

The air conditioner refused again to make it through the night. I understand so well how difficult it is to function properly in extreme heat and sympathize with the wall-mounted machine. I decide that we should all have a breaker system that switches us off when we hit overload.

I smile at my early rising. It pleases me as it allows me to watch the town wake up in peaceful slowness without the hustle of peddlers, tourists, gigolos, workers, tour buses, beggars, traffic, opportunists – without all this reality. Only too soon the sidewalks will be lined with goods, mannequins overpowering the walkways, men and young boys calling attention to whatever they are selling. I can hear it even before it begins. It is an integral part of survival here, where tourists pick and choose depending on the best act, the brightest smile, the nicest-looking waiter or the most promising prices.

The silent breeze is welcome now, to be turned off by nature itself in an hour. The sun will beam and even at half strength will eradicate any semblance of coolness. A hot furnace will blow off the marina, delighting the palm and banana trees. I imagine them opening to the puffs of air and swaying gently. For now they are stolid, in repose from the evening's activity of being hugged, climbed, photographed and tugged at, all the while attempting to handle the salt washes.

Scents of coffee and yeast fill my nostrils. I follow my nose with the hope that it will lead to a place to sit and study, undisturbed; to wake at a leisurely pace while examining, for the twenty-third consecutive day, the bases and basics of

*City Beach – Monoprint with chine colle*

this foreign culture and its history and people. The likelihood of no interference is slim, based on recent experience. Each day, however, I change my route in an attempt to find a place that honours my request and caters to my sensibilities. Searching for a haven along with scenery that will fulfill my hope that this part of Eden does, in fact, exist and produces bountiful goodness. I am naive ; a bit innocent. I am not likely to change.

Armed with fifteen vital "to dos" on my quickly scribbled but well-thought-out list, I venture out to see them all accomplished. One remains elusive. The one closest to my heart. The one that is the most difficult to recognize as finalized. The one I believed I'd found so many times only to be disillusioned by the truth. It is the one that catapults me into this area of the world for the third time in as many years. I know it is here. I feel it and so I am compelled to continue my pursuit. I am in search of my faith in humanity. I lost it somewhere along life's path. It remains essential to my nourishment. Time convinces me that I cannot live without that faith as I am fading. Determination will prevail, I am tepidly certain.

Coming so close to the completion of my list has at once inspired and frustrated me. Recent visits have produced close results. The mosques, the churches, the ruins in distant communities, speaking with the inhabitants, touching history, the air, the sea, the colours – all allowing for the universe to work, have cumulatively led me back. All these avenues ventured, producing more and more yearning in my soul; a higher need for exactness and a resolve not to be suppressed or, even worse, wrong in my instincts.

Friends back home know about my quest. They do not know details, but they still understand. I am not so sure that I would be as understanding and so I respect and love them more for their blind support. I wonder if envy of my wanderings led to their acceptance. I am quite certain that nobody's list matches mine. Therefore, they must each have their own list and imagine mine to be similar. Yes, that is the reason for the giggles, the hugs and the pure feeling of sisterhood. I picture for a moment their reaction to the poem I wrote. Now, some call me "the gypsy." My ego is placated by the nickname. It sets me apart and gives me wings of power. It substantiates this journey, if only to my own conscience.

*Orange Scape – Water colour, oil pastel*

*I find myself reciting the poem out loud, knowing that the words were one of the things that sent me here. I am careful to use a soft voice. The least attention I attract the better chance I have of drinking that cup of coffee alone and perhaps accomplishing my final task. Today may be the day.*

*When the winds of change*
*Grow silent*
*And the gypsy*
*Is confused...........*

*.........Perhaps this day*
*She'll take*
*Her leave*
*And*
*Feel her freedom*
*Once again*

*Or perhaps*
*Enjoy just*
*One more night*
*In her*
*Environment*
*So strange.*

*By the time I finish my private recital, tears well in me, uncontrolled. The verses hit a nerve. The words represent me and are deeply personal. My oversized, unnecessary sunglasses disguise my emotions and I don't bother wiping my face. Hopefully the stream of tears will not leave a crust on my skin as I have seen on children.*

*The Docks (reminder of a place) - Monoprint*

*Looking up to my angels and watching them guide me on my way today as usual helps break the lump in my throat. Calmness and clarity take over, and I silently acknowledge their presence. I thank them with my smile and through my newly dry eyes. Being distracted by my emotions causes me to let my guard down for a fraction of time. A fraction is all that is needed, obviously. I kick myself for indulging in daydreams and poetry recitals, taking my sights off my surroundings. Perhaps I am paying the price for satisfying my ego.*

*Standing in my space, so close I can feel his breath leave moisture droplets on my hair, is a stranger – and a big one at that. All I can see is his shirt buttons. He smells clean, his skin seems tanned, his belly flat and muscular. I do not dare look up or down. My primary instincts set in as I choose not to move a muscle. If this was a wild predator, how would I behave? I am in the wild, confronted by a ferocious beast, perhaps a lion...I will not stir. The hair stands up on my arms with dread of what might happen. There is not a soul in sight. The sun is only now ever-so-slightly peeking through the darkness, and I seem to have gone off track. I am unsure of my whereabouts as the pavement has turned to cobblestone. Stupid, stupid, stupid, dumb. I beat myself up –not the first time on this trip.*

*The standoff continues far past expectations. Neither he nor I move a muscle. I cannot, for the life of me (perhaps literally?), figure out what to do or say. All I know is that my emotions are rising. I am unable to decide if I am more annoyed, frightened, curious or amused. It is a ridiculous, unnatural stance. My face sets on fire as I imagine everyone looking.*

*Time passes. I suddenly feel my shoulders start to shake, as do those of my predator. Silly laughter escapes us simultaneously. We take a giant step back in tandem.*

*I evaluate him carefully.*

*He has a nice face. His laugh is deep and real. It creeps into his eyes. I am thinking how extremely attractive he is. I am stupid, stupid, stupid, dumb.*

*My mystery man finally speaks first revealing warm, soft tones in slightly accented English. He has my full attention, and so, in spite of myself, I reveal my attentiveness, almost leaning forward to hear him. He has yet to introduce himself. I feel he knows my name therefore I don't bother with introductions either. They would seem out of place.*

"I have watched you for days. You walk three times, always after the call for prayer. You are searching for something.... I have walked beside you, behind you, raced farther ahead and watched you pass. You have not been aware of my existence. Now, tell me this: You are obviously looking for something. How do you intend to find it when you insist on looking straight ahead? Even when you rest or drink or eat, your back is straight, as is your gaze. Will you tell me what you hope to find using this manner of search?"

The residual of my prior burst of spontaneous laughter subsides, as does any humour. This is not amusing at all. I am curious, though, as the unravelling of this odd event intrigues me enough to feel compelled to answer back truthfully. Incredulously, I truly do not remember spotting him follow me. I give myself a failing grade for not noticing him. Here I was thinking I was so tuned into my surroundings and environment. What a joke I am. I decide that he deserves a response since he is right about my search. I am seeking something – he is definitely right. Suddenly I am feeling very solemn and trusting. I begin slowly, deliberate with my words, my voice steady and clear.

"I am simply looking for my faith in humanity. I know it was with me at one time but it is now somewhere in my past. And I don't ever look back. I know it does not walk beside me. I don't feel it there. Therefore, I conclude it must be directly up ahead, but I seem unable to recognize it. It might be unrecoverable. That is a tragedy I cannot live with. If I do not find it, my spirit will die." Not that anyone should care, I add silently. I am still very confounded at his role in my quest. I am still confounded by the whole experience.

The sun chooses this exact moment to make its daily debut.

The stranger shifts his stance, pivoting to stand in line with me, eyes facing straight ahead. He holds my hand, our arms grazing, and I do not pull away. His hand is large, cool to the touch, slightly calloused and a comfortable fit. I feel warmth and safety in his touch, like a protected child.

Our eyes collectively follow what appears to be a bright, narrow torch. I realize that it is one of the sun's rays.

We are close to the water's edge. How did I get to be here? The atmosphere is surreal, and I am tempted to pinch myself. I forget about finding an open café or escaping this situation. I forget to think at all. Instead, I let a feeling of *contentment wash over me, mixing with the gentle sea breeze. It is the most natural place on earth for me to be right now.*

*Urban – Sea    Twin Monoprint*

Mentally I am preparing myself for something special. My instincts have never been stronger as I play with words like "destiny," "miracle," "once in a lifetime…" I pray to God not to disappoint me. I thank him too, just in case I am ultimately disappointed and cannot bring myself to give thanks later. I equate the situation with receiving a beautifully wrapped gift that disguises an unwanted item. I leave out the second part, though, and stick with simple thanks. My faith is teetering, but this remains my secret. I don't want God to know just yet.

As we watch the ray of light, my companion answers my silent question.

"They will go out again after this to fish all day, providing food and income for their own families. By six this evening, they will return to pick up staple supplies donated in rotation by the shopkeepers in town. They will have a lot of help unloading their gear and fish from the boat, exchanging the space for the treasured supplies. Under the cover of darkness, each of these seven tiny boats will drop off the cases and bags of food and water and, at the same time, pick up children, women and elderly refugees. They will spread their human cargo evenly between the boats and follow separate routes back here. This has been a weekly event for several months now…about eighty percent of the region is involved in some capacity. The refugee centre and school are in the mountains. Tomorrow I will take you there."

With his final word, the beam of sunlight expands just enough to outline the figures in the semi-darkness and confirms it as truth. I am overwhelmed and humbled by the sight, choosing for the second time this morning not to wipe my tears.

His grip tightens as we again follow the scent of coffee and yeast. We smile together, not broadly, not tightly, just authentically. Our eyes meet with ease as though we have been acquainted for a long time.

As we stroll, I do a pirouette. His hand raises, guiding me very slowly on my three-hundred-and-sixty-degree spin. My skirt obeys me and lifts slightly, causing me to feel even more lightness in my steps. I swallow the tremendous beauty of the mountains, valleys and sea and all its vessels, most still tucked in for the night. The citrus, grape and pomegranate orchards and ancient ruins that occupy the luscious landscape are illuminated by the pinkish morning light. I turn farther to see the simple homes and the people who have restored me.

As I look around for the very first time, I know solidly that the gypsy has found her place. It is in Eden.

"But now it is time to depart – for me to die, for you to live. But which of us it going to a better state is unknown to everyone but God." Plato

# Notes from the Author

My poems and artwork are a product that came into being as a direct result of listening. There were no intricate schemes involved. No wondering if I was getting it right. No need for worries or for doubt. Nothing lay between myself and the emotion put into my craft. Listening has afforded me diversity, understanding and a deeper knowledge of myself and others. Sharing naturally completes the process. I thank you all.

The four years spent compiling this book have likely been the most challenging years to date in my life. At this time I would like to acknowledge and thank those who have supported, cajoled, laughed, danced, listened and cried with me along the way. Big thanks to those I have met from all parts of the world who educated and charmed me as well as those who joined me in my adventures if only in their imaginations and in my heart. While they may have been the most challenging times I feel certain they will also be held in my memory as being some of the most fulfilling.

This idea of this book at inception was triggered by a quote that said, (translated) "I cracked my heart for every time I laughed in my life"

… a statement that ended with:

"In spite of all that I love life." - Of which I thought – **Hey! That sounds like me!**

*Wadi Rum – Jordan, 2010 (photo Bruce Braine, Toronto)*

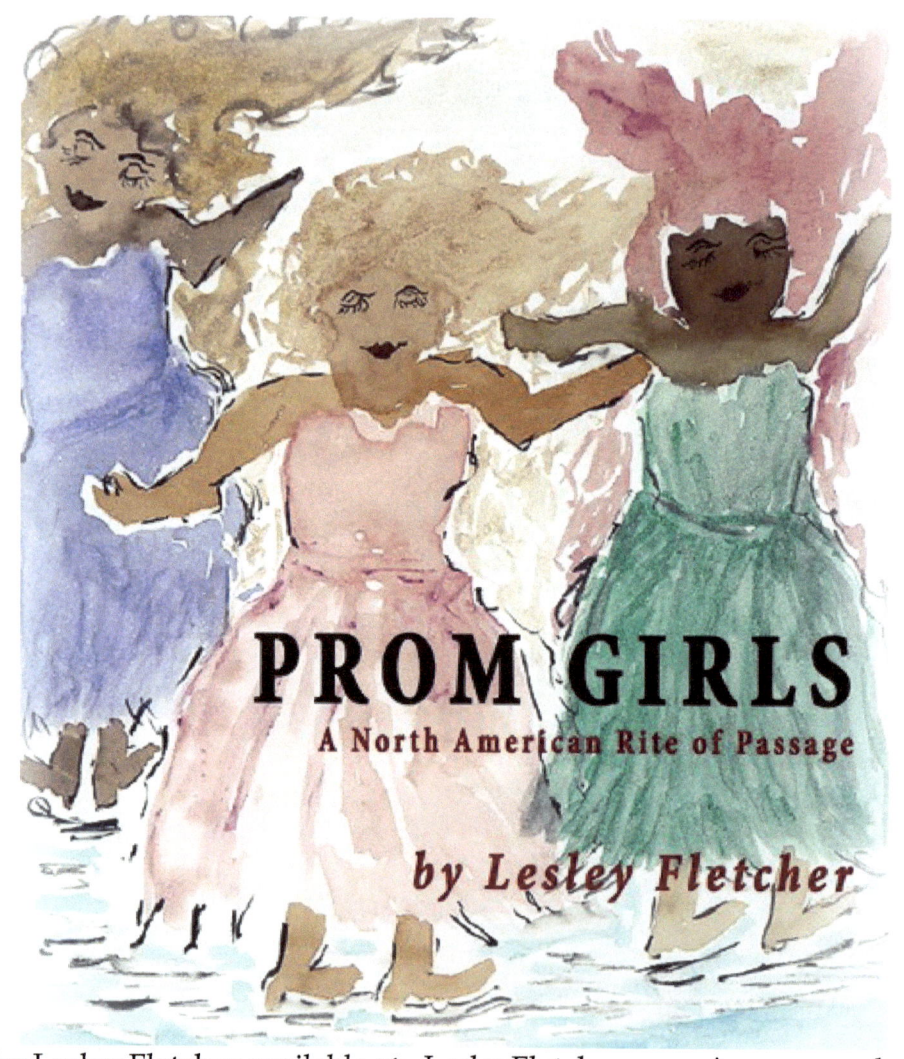

Other books by Lesley Fletcher available at LesleyFletcher.com, Amazon and other retailers.

To learn more about the Author please visit LesleyFletcher.com There you will find ways to connect, view art, and purchase her books and artwork.

**INSPIRED READERS: STEP TWO**

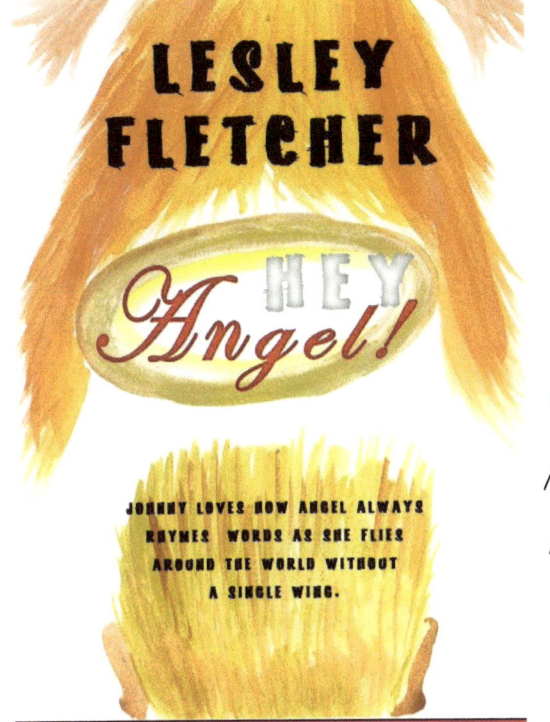

**INSPIRED READERS: PRE-K**

*If you enjoy reading this or one of my other books and viewing my artwork please say so by tweeting, liking or leaving feedback or a review. As an independent artist and writer it is truly appreciated. Thank you very much!*

*Peace, Lesley*